DETROIT LIONS

by Matt Tustison

Printed in the United States of America,
North Mankato, Minnesota
062010
092010

♻ THIS BOOK CONTAINS AT LEAST 10% RECYCLED MATERIALS.

Editor: Chrös McDougall
Copy Editor: Nicholas Cafarelli
Interior Design and Production: Craig Hinton
Cover Design: Craig Hinton

Photo Credits: Greg Trott/AP Images, cover; David Stluka/AP Images, title page, 47; AP Images, 4, 14, 20, 24, 33, 42 (middle), 43 (top); Vernon Biever/Getty Images, 7, 42 (bottom); Frank Rippon/NFL/Getty Images, 9; NFL Photos/AP Images, 10, 22, 29, 42 (top); Fox/AP Images, 13; George Gelatly/NFL/Getty Images, 17, 18; John Stormzand/AP Images, 26; Tom Pidgeon/AP Images, 30; Morry Gash/AP Images, 34, 43 (middle); Paul Sancya/AP Images, 37, 38, 41, 43 (bottom); Paul Jasienski/AP Images, 44

Library of Congress Cataloging-in-Publication Data
Tustison, Matt, 1978-
  Detroit Lions / Matt Tustison.
    p. cm. — (Inside the NFL)
  Includes index.
  ISBN 978-1-61714-011-2
  1. Detroit Lions (Football team)—History—Juvenile literature. I. Title.
  GV956.D4T87 2010
  796.332'640977434—dc22
                            2010018843

TABLE OF CONTENTS

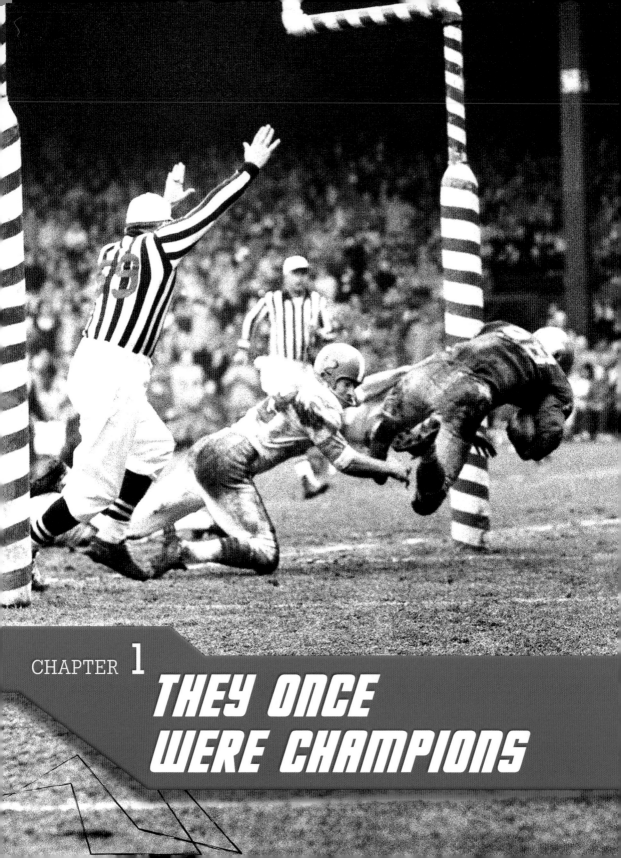

CHAPTER 1

THEY ONCE WERE CHAMPIONS

T he Detroit Lions finished the 1957 season with a mighty roar. On December 29 of that year, they crushed the Cleveland Browns 59–14 and won the National Football League (NFL) Championship Game.

Lions quarterback Tobin Rote threw for four touchdowns and ran for one. He completed 12 of 19 passes for 280 yards. Detroit held Cleveland's star running back Jim Brown to 69 rushing yards on 20 carries. The 55,263 fans in attendance at Briggs Stadium in Detroit were proud of their Lions.

BUDDY PARKER

Lions coach Buddy Parker came up with many innovations. He was the first coach to have his squad stay together in a hotel the night before home games. This was done to help the team focus on the coming game without any distractions. He shortened practices, loosened rules for players, and was credited with starting the "two-minute offense." In the two-minute offense, the team lines up without huddling or by huddling quickly. This allows for more plays when the time is running out.

LIONS TIGHT END STEVE JUNKER DIVES INTO THE END ZONE FOR A TOUCHDOWN DURING THE 1957 NFL CHAMPIONSHIP GAME.

TOBIN ROTE

Quarterback Tobin Rote was selected seventeenth overall by the Green Bay Packers in the 1950 NFL Draft. During his six years in Green Bay, he ranked third in the NFL in passing touchdowns and first in rushing yards by a quarterback. In 1956, the Packers went 4–8. But Rote led the league in passing yards (2,203) and touchdowns (18). He also rushed for 11 touchdowns.

After the 1956 season, Green Bay traded Rote to Detroit. Rote shared playing time with Bobby Layne with the Lions in 1957. But after Layne was injured late in the season, Rote took over on a full-time basis and led Detroit to the NFL title. Rote was the starter for two more years with the Lions. He then played several more seasons in the Canadian Football League and the American Football League (AFL). He retired after playing for the AFL's Denver Broncos in 1966.

The 1957 season had actually started with a shock for Detroit. Buddy Parker had coached the Lions to NFL titles in 1952 and 1953. But before the 1957 season, he announced he was quitting.

"I have a situation here I cannot handle. This is the worst team in training camp I have ever seen," he said during a banquet just before the season. "I don't want to get involved in another losing season, so I'm leaving Detroit football. I'm leaving tonight."

And he did.

The Lions named George Wilson the new head coach. He had been the team's ends and backs coach. Most people, including Detroit's players, liked Wilson. But few people had confidence in him as a head coach in the NFL.

LINEBACKER JOE SCHMIDT RUNS WITH THE BALL IN A 20–6 WIN OVER THE GREEN BAY PACKERS IN 1956.

Rote was also new to the team in 1957. He had been traded to the Lions from the Green Bay Packers. In Detroit, Rote shared the quarterback duties with Bobby Layne. Layne had led the Lions at that position since 1950.

Layne was very popular in Detroit. However, the Lions had missed a conference title in 1956 in part because Layne had gotten hurt in the season finale against the Chicago Bears. That led to Detroit's decision to acquire Rote. Layne was not happy to be sharing the position.

Detroit started out the 1957 season 6–4. The Lions were in the race for the conference title with two games left. The next game was against Cleveland at Briggs Stadium. In the second quarter, Layne dropped back to pass. But the Browns' Don Colo and Paul Wiggin smashed into Layne. Several bones were broken in his ankle and lower leg. Rote took over at quarterback. He led Detroit to a 20–7 win at Cleveland.

The Lions then went on to beat the Bears 21–13 in the regular-season finale. That put Detroit in a tie with the San Francisco 49ers for the NFL Western Conference title. The teams played a one-game play-off to decide which one would advance to the NFL Championship Game. The visiting Lions rallied to beat the 49ers 31–27.

Detroit followed that victory with the big title-game win over Cleveland. It was a joyous time in Michigan. Unfortunately, Lions fans are still waiting for their team to match that level of success. Through 2009, the Lions had still not won another NFL championship, which is now called the Super Bowl. In fact, Detroit won only one playoff game in that time.

One postseason victory in more than 50 seasons—it is one of the most frustrating and least successful stretches of play for a team in NFL history.

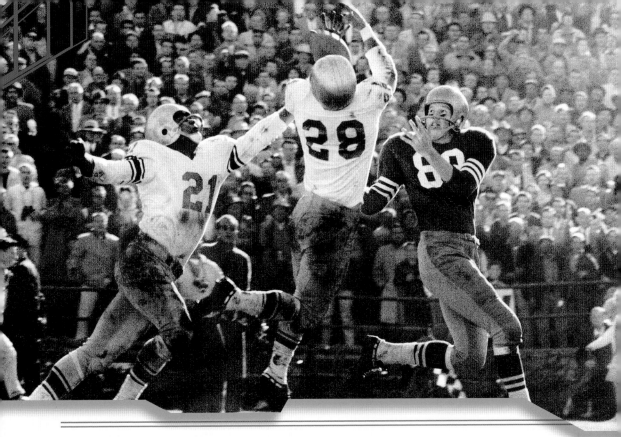

LIONS DEFENSIVE BACK YALE LARY (28) BREAKS UP A PASS DURING THE 1957 NFL WESTERN CONFERENCE TITLE GAME.

At one time the Lions were one of the most feared teams in the league. They won their first NFL title in 1935—only their second year playing in Detroit. The Lions then won the league title in 1952, 1953, and 1957.

Despite having some excellent players, Detroit has not enjoyed much team success in the 50-plus years that have followed. That was not what radio executive George A. Richards had in mind when he purchased the Portsmouth (Ohio) Spartans in 1934 for a then-astounding $8,000 and moved the team to Detroit.

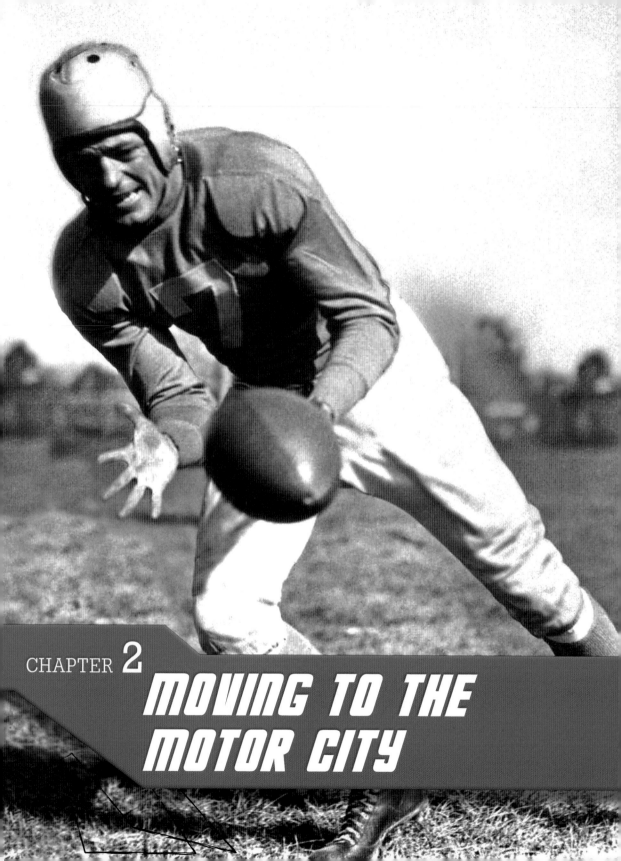

CHAPTER 2

MOVING TO THE MOTOR CITY

The Portsmouth Spartans were formed in Portsmouth, Ohio, in 1929. The Spartans would later move to Detroit and become the Lions. The Spartans were an independent team in the Ohio and Scioto River Valleys for their first season. They gained membership in the young NFL for the 1930 season.

The Spartans and the Chicago Bears ended the 1932 season tied with six wins each. The NFL championship had previously been awarded to the team with the best record in the league. But since the Spartans and the Bears were tied, they played each other in the first NFL title game.

IRON MAN GAME

Portsmouth played an "iron man" game against Green Bay in 1932. Spartans coach Potsy Clark refused to make a single substitution. Portsmouth won 19–0 while using only 11 players.

Chicago beat Portsmouth 9–0 to win the league title. After that, the league created

EARL "DUTCH" CLARK PLAYED FOR THE DETROIT LIONS FROM 1934 TO 1938. CLARK WAS INDUCTED INTO THE PRO FOOTBALL HALL OF FAME IN 1963.

Eastern and Western divisions. The division winners began playing in the regular NFL Championship Game in 1933.

The Spartans were successful on the field. But the country was suffering from the Great Depression. Teams were making less money because few people could afford to attend games. Some teams went out of business. Detroit radio executive George A. Richards saw this as an opportunity. He bought the Spartans and moved the team to Detroit. He renamed the team the Lions because he wanted them to be the kings of the NFL.

The Lions won their first NFL title in 1935. It was only their second season in Detroit. Freezing rain had turned University of Detroit Stadium into a muddy mess. But the Lions beat the New York Giants 26–7. Quarterback Earl "Dutch" Clark led the way for Detroit. He ran for a 40-yard touchdown. Clark was considered a triple threat on offense—he was an effective passer, runner, and drop kicker.

Clark became a member of the Pro Football Hall of Fame's first class of inductees in 1963. He played for the Lions until 1938. During his final two seasons, he also served as the team's head coach. He was known for his cool-headed leadership.

The Lions enjoyed some early success during their first several seasons in Detroit in the 1930s. The 1940s were more challenging. They won only 35 of 111 games during the decade.

In 1942, Detroit went 0–11. The team had only five touchdowns all season and did not score more than seven points in any game. In 1943, the host Lions played the Giants in a

LIONS DEFENDER JACK MATHESON TACKLES BOSTON YANKS HALFBACK
JOHNNY GRIGAS DURING A SNOWY 10–9 VICTORY IN 1945.

game that ended in a 0–0 tie. Through 2009, that was the last scoreless tie in the NFL.

The Lions managed winning seasons in 1944 and 1945. They went 6–3–1 in 1944 and 7–3 in 1945. But from 1946 to 1949, the Lions won just a total of 10 games. The team's fans were looking forward to a new decade. The 1950s would turn out to be much more successful.

PASS THE TURKEY

The Lions scheduled a game on Thanksgiving Day in 1934. They lost 19–16 to visiting Chicago. But the Lions continued playing the Bears on Thanksgiving through 1938. Detroit stopped the turkey day tradition for a while. But the Lions picked it back up with a 28–21 win over the Cleveland Rams on Thanksgiving Day 1945. Detroit has played on every Thanksgiving Day since. In 1966, the Dallas Cowboys also started a Thanksgiving game tradition. Dallas has played on every Thanksgiving Day since, except two. The Lions and Cowboys always play at home as part of this special tradition.

CHAPTER 3

THE ROARING FIFTIES

In 1950, the Lions drafted running back Doak Walker. They also picked up quarterback Bobby Layne in a trade with the New York Bulldogs. Layne and Walker were old friends. They had lived in the same neighborhood and even attended the same high school in Dallas, Texas. They had also been college rivals.

However, the 1950 season did not go well. The Lions finished 6–6. Coach Alvin "Bo" McMillin resigned afterward. Assistant Buddy Parker was promoted to head coach. He had played for the Lions as a fullback. He even helped them win the 1935 NFL title.

"He was one coach who never forgot he was a player," Bobby Layne said. "He treated the players like adults. He expected you to do the job, period. You could tell that first year that something special was happening."

Layne was right. Detroit's greatest era had begun.

DOAK WALKER JOINED THE LIONS IN 1950. TODAY, THE DOAK WALKER AWARD HONORS THE NATION'S TOP COLLEGE RUNNING BACK EACH YEAR.

The Los Angeles Rams won the National Conference and NFL titles in 1951. The Lions finished only a half-game behind the Rams. With a 7–4–1 record, they tied for second place with the San Francisco 49ers.

Detroit finally got back to the NFL Championship Game after the 1952 season. After a shaky 1–2 start that season, they won nine of their final 10 games in the regular season. The Rams and Lions each finished with 9–3 records.

The visiting Lions beat the Rams 31–21 in a playoff game. Then they played the Cleveland Browns in the NFL Championship Game. The title game took place on December 28. In subfreezing temperatures, the visiting Lions faced the Browns and star quarterback Otto Graham. Early in the second quarter, Layne scored on a 2-yard run. Then, in the third quarter, Walker had a touchdown on a fine 67-yard scamper. That gave Detroit a 14–0 lead.

Cleveland's Chick Jagade found the end zone on a 7-yard run in the third quarter. That brought the Browns within seven points. But Harder added a 36-yard field goal in the fourth quarter to put Detroit ahead 17–7. The Lions held on to win by that score, giving them their second NFL title. The Lions did not slow down after that.

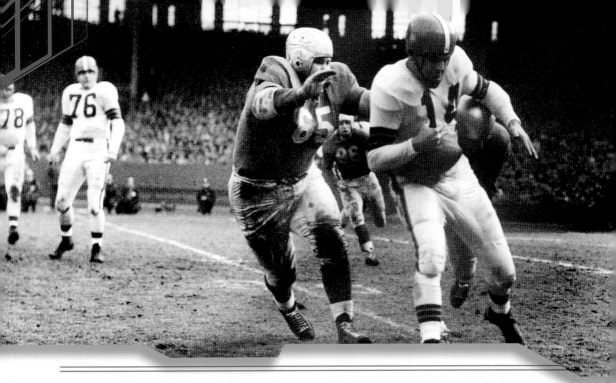

TWO LIONS BRING DOWN CLEVELAND BROWNS QUARTERBACK OTTO GRAHAM DURING THE 1952 NFL CHAMPIONSHIP GAME.

They started 4–2 in 1953. Then they won their final six games to finish with a 10–2 record and win the Western Conference title. Detroit again faced Cleveland for the NFL title.

The 1953 NFL Championship Game was at Briggs Stadium. It turned out to be one of the league's all-time best. The score was tied at 10 after three quarters. The Browns kicked two field goals to take a 16–10 lead. With 4:10 left, the Lions started at their own 20-yard line. Layne moved Detroit to Cleveland's 33. Layne then found Jim Doran for a perfectly thrown 33-yard touchdown pass with 2:08 remaining. Walker kicked the extra point to give Detroit a 17–16 lead. Detroit held on to win by that score.

Parker gave credit to Layne for the Lions' second straight

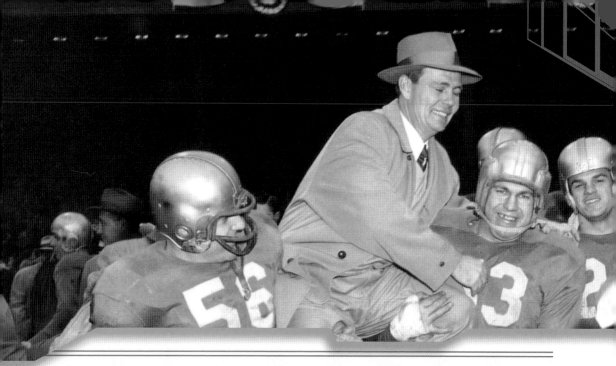

LINEBACKER JOE SCHMIDT, *LEFT*, AND TACKLE LOU CREEKMUR CARRY COACH BUDDY PARKER OFF THE FIELD AFTER THE 1953 NFL CHAMPIONSHIP GAME.

NFL title. "You may win five or six games a season with an ordinary player at quarterback, but as far as the title is concerned, you might as well stay at home if you don't have the real big guy at the spot," Parker said. "We did."

The next season, the Lions finished 9–2–1 and won the Western Conference crown. They met Cleveland again in the NFL title game. This time, though, the host Browns dominated the favored Lions 56–10.

Layne hurt his right shoulder before the 1955 season and had trouble throwing. Several Lions retired. The team finished last in the Western Conference with an NFL-worst 3–9 record.

Walker retired after the 1955 season. But Layne was back on target. The Lions won their first six games in 1956. They visited the Chicago Bears in the final week of the regular season. The game decided the Western Conference champion. Chicago won 38–21 and earned the title. Layne had been knocked out by a hit from behind. He did not come out of his haze until the second half.

Layne's injury led Detroit to trade for quarterback Tobin Rote before the 1957 season. Parker quit as coach before that season and was replaced by George Wilson. The Lions went on to win their third NFL championship of the decade.

Layne was determined to play in 1958. In the second game of the season, Detroit nearly defeated Green Bay. Instead, they tied 13–13. Layne missed an extra point that would have given Detroit the win. Layne received a call from Wilson on Monday. He had been traded to

the Steelers. Layne boarded a plane that night and was in Pittsburgh for practice on Tuesday.

On his way out of Detroit, Layne reportedly said the Lions would "not win for 50 years." This prediction proved to be true, as far as NFL titles go. It is called the "Curse of Bobby Layne." Detroit finished 4–7–1 in 1958 and dropped to 3–8–1 the next year. "You could see the trade upset the club," linebacker Wayne Walker said. "It all went downhill after that."

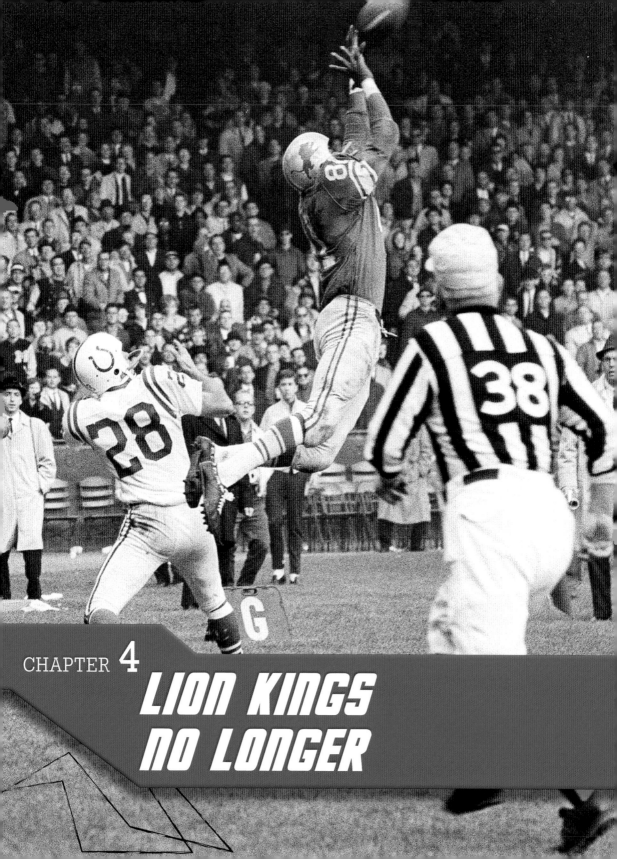

CHAPTER **4**

LION KINGS NO LONGER

Star quarterback Bobby Layne was not a Detroit Lion anymore. But that did not stop the team from winning. The Lions finished second in the Western Conference in 1960, 1961, and 1962. During those years, defense was Detroit's strength.

Linebacker Joe Schmidt was so aggressive that he was nicknamed "Red Dog." Safety Yale Lary made 50 interceptions during his career with the Lions. Cornerback Dick "Night Train" Lane was known for hitting the opposition ball carriers high and hard. But perhaps the most frightening Lion was 270-pound defensive tackle Alex Karras. He was strong, relentless, and very fast. Offensive linemen feared him. Sometimes even running backs could not match his speed.

"Running away from Karras is worse than running at him," Baltimore Colts running back Lenny Moore said. "He moves so fast on those stumpy legs, and you can hear him closing in

DICK "NIGHT TRAIN" LANE LEAPS TO BREAK UP A PASS INTENDED FOR BALTIMORE COLTS RECEIVER JIMMY ORR DURING A 1962 WIN.

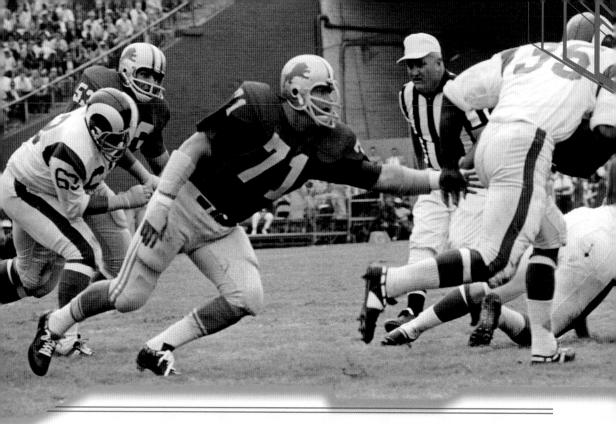

LIONS DEFENSIVE TACKLE ALEX KARRAS REACHES OUT TO TACKLE A
LOS ANGELES RAMS PLAYER DURING THE LIONS' 10–7 LOSS IN 1968.

on you from behind. I hate that sound. You get this feeling like you're about to be buried by a buffalo stampede."

The Lions drafted Karras in 1958. Just before that, he had signed a professional wrestling contract. That earned him $25,000 during the six-month off-season.

Karras's wrestling background came in handy again in 1963. That January, the NFL questioned his ownership in the Lindell AC Bar in Detroit. There had been reports on the bar of gambling and the influence of organized crime. Karras was urged to sell his piece of the business. He first threatened to retire from football. He then admitted to placing bets on NFL games. The league suspended him for one season. Karras returned to pro wrestling for the year. One of his famous wrestling opponents was "Dick the Bruiser."

NFL commissioner Pete Rozelle reinstated Karras for the 1964 season. During that season, an official asked Karras to call the pregame coin toss for his team. "I'm sorry, sir," Karras replied. "I'm not permitted to gamble."

Karras verbally sparred with the Lions' coaches. He asked to be traded in 1964. He threatened to sign with the expansion Miami Dolphins of the American Football League (AFL) in 1966. He then hinted that he might retire. But through it all, he remained with Detroit.

The Lions of the 1960s had several other talented players

PAPER LION

In 1963, sportswriter George Plimpton joined the Lions for their training camp at Cranbrook, a boys' private school near Bloomfield Hills, Michigan. The result of his experiences is chronicled in the book Paper Lion: Confessions of a Last-String Quarterback. Plimpton wore No. 0 and participated in a Lions scrimmage at Wisner Stadium in Pontiac, Michigan. He netted minus-29 yards in his five plays at quarterback. Plimpton, then 36 years old, showed how difficult it would be for an average person to succeed in the NFL. The book is considered a sports literature classic.

besides Karras, even if they did not make as many newspaper headlines. Dick LeBeau and, later in the decade, Lem Barney were standout defensive backs. Both would be enshrined in the Pro Football Hall of Fame. So would tight end Charlie Sanders. The team had drafted him in 1968. Linebacker Wayne Walker and center Ed Flanagan were other players who received frequent Pro Bowl selections.

LIONS RUNNING BACK BILLY SIMS RUSHED FOR 153 YARDS AND THREE TOUCHDOWNS IN HIS FIRST PRO GAME IN 1980.

THE SILVERDOME

The Lions played their final game at Tiger Stadium on Thanksgiving Day of 1974. They moved to the newly built Pontiac Silverdome for the 1975 season. Pontiac is a suburb of Detroit. The Silverdome was the Lions' home through 2001. The stadium sat 80,311 fans for football. When it was built, the stadium cost $55.7 million. In 2009, it was sold at auction for a winning bid of just $583,000.

Detroit had several losing seasons in the 1960s, however. The Lions did not reach the play-offs during the entire decade. The 1970s would not be much different.

The Lions only made the playoffs once in the 1970s, and that was in 1970. Detroit lost

5–0 to the Dallas Cowboys in the first round. That was the lowest-scoring playoff game in NFL history. From 1970 to 1978, the Lions placed either second or third every year in their division.

In 1979, Detroit finished with the worst record in the league at 2–14. That gave the team the first pick in the 1980 NFL Draft. The Lions used the pick to select Heisman Trophy-winning running back Billy Sims from the University of Oklahoma. Sims was named the NFL Rookie of the Year in 1980. He rushed for a team-record 1,303 yards and scored 16 touchdowns total. Thirteen were rushing and three receiving.

With Sims leading the way, the Lions made the playoffs in 1982 and 1983. They went 9–7 and won the National Football Conference (NFC) Central Division in 1983. Detroit lost in the

MOTOWN AND THE LIONS

In 1970, Marvin Gaye, a star pop/rhythm and blues singer for Motown Records in Detroit, decided to fulfill a dream. He gained weight and trained for a tryout with the Lions. He was cut quickly. He remained friends with many players, though. Fullback Mel Farr and cornerback Lem Barney appeared as vocalists on Gaye's classic 1971 song, "What's Going On."

first round of the postseason both times. The host Washington Redskins beat Detroit 31–7 in 1982. The host San Francisco 49ers and quarterback Joe Montana edged the Lions 24–23 in the wild-card round in 1983. Detroit's Eddie Murray missed a 43-yard field-goal try with five seconds left.

Sims suffered a knee injury in 1984. This ended his career just as it was taking off. It also hurt Detroit's prospects of success. The Lions would not manage a record over .500 for the rest of the decade.

CHAPTER 5

BARRY'S BUNCH

In the 1989 NFL Draft, the Lions selected running back Barry Sanders with the third overall pick. He helped make the 1990s one of the most interesting and successful decades in team history. Detroit reached the playoffs six times during the decade. With his incredible running ability, Sanders became known as one of the best running backs in NFL history.

Sanders had earned the Heisman Trophy for his 1988 season at Oklahoma State University. He rushed for a college-record 2,628 yards and scored 39 touchdowns. Sanders was only 5-foot-8. But he had a combination of great balance, vision, and strength. His ability to spin, juke, and cut was unmatched in the game.

"Barry is so good that sometimes during a game, I catch myself watching as a fan and not an opponent," former Tampa Bay

RUNNING BACK BARRY SANDERS, *RIGHT*, HOLDS UP HIS NEW DETROIT LIONS JERSEY WITH TEAM EXECUTIVE CHUCK SCHMIDT AFTER THE LIONS SELECTED SANDERS THIRD IN THE 1989 NFL DRAFT.

HUMBLE HERO

Lions running back Barry Sanders decided to wear No. 20 as a rookie. Former star running back Billy Sims had worn that same number with Detroit. Sanders rushed for 1,470 yards in 1989, breaking Sims's team record for a first-year player. Sanders finished 10 yards short of the NFL rushing title in his rookie season.

Kansas City's Christian Okoye had 1,480 yards that year. Sanders could have won the rushing title in the final game of the season. But he chose not to go back into a game that the Lions had control of in the fourth quarter. "Coach, let's just win it and go home," he reportedly said.

Despite being one of the NFL's top players, Sanders did not have a big ego. He was known for politely handing the ball to a referee after he scored touchdowns instead of calling attention to himself with a celebratory dance.

Buccaneers linebacker Hardy Nickerson said. "He does things that leave even pros' mouths hanging open."

Sanders finished with 1,470 rushing yards in 1989. He was chosen as NFL Rookie of the Year. Sanders also broke Billy Sims's Lions rookie rushing record. He went on to rush for a combined 8,672 yards in his first six years in the NFL. He was selected to the Pro Bowl in each of those seasons. Many fans loved his elusive running style.

Two-sport star Bo Jackson played running back for the Los Angeles Raiders and outfield for the Kansas City Royals. Even he admired Sanders. Jackson said, "When I grow up, I want to be just like him. Barry's my new idol. I like the way he runs. He's a water bug out there the way he moves."

BARRY SANDERS HAD 69 RUSHING YARDS AND A TOUCHDOWN IN THE
LIONS' 1991 PLAYOFF WIN OVER THE DALLAS COWBOYS.

Detroit strengthened the rest of the team around Sanders. The defense included talented linebackers Chris Spielman, Pat Swilling, and Tracy Scroggins. Bennie Blades was a hard-hitting safety. Sanders had a seven-time Pro Bowl player, Lomas Brown, at tackle to open holes for him. At wide receiver, Brett Perriman combined speed with precise route running. And Herman Moore had been an outstanding high jumper on the University

QUARTERBACK SCOTT MITCHELL GETS RID OF THE BALL BEFORE A MINNESOTA VIKINGS DEFENDER TACKLES HIM DURING A 1995 GAME.

A BIG "THUMBS UP"

On November 17, 1991, Lions guard Mike Utley suffered a career-ending paralysis injury in a game against the Los Angeles Rams. As Utley was carted off the field, he flashed a "thumbs up" to his teammates and the crowd at the Silverdome. This became a rallying symbol for the remainder of the season.

of Virginia track and field team. At 6-foot-4, the wide receiver was able to outleap defenders for high passes.

With these players, the Lions ended a long period of mediocrity. The 1991 team picked up the team's first play-off victory since 1957. Detroit defeated visiting Dallas 38–6 in a divisional-round game on January 5, 1992. But Detroit lost the next week, 41–10 to the host Washington Redskins in the NFC Championship Game. Washington would go on to win the Super Bowl.

The 1993 Lions lost 28–24 to the visiting Green Bay Packers in a wild-card playoff game. Sanders rushed for 169 yards. But the Packers won on a 40-yard fourth-quarter touchdown pass from Brett Favre to Sterling Sharpe.

Before the 1994 season, the Lions signed quarterback Scott Mitchell. Mitchell had been a backup with the Miami Dolphins. Coach Wayne Fontes named him as the Lions' starter. Mitchell struggled in the 1994 season, though. The Lions were

OFFENSIVE FIREWORKS

The Lions' offense excelled in 1995. Detroit gained 6,113 yards for the season, the most in the NFL. Wide receiver Herman Moore set an NFL record with 123 receptions. His 1,686 receiving yards and Brett Perriman's 1,488 combined for the most ever (3,174) by a pair of NFL teammates. Barry Sanders, meanwhile, rushed for exactly 1,500 yards. Scott Mitchell threw 32 touchdown passes, breaking Bobby Layne's team mark of 26. Unfortunately for the Lions, even their great offense could not overcome poor defensive play in their 58–37 playoff loss to the Philadelphia Eagles.

5–6 at the beginning of December. Mitchell was replaced by veteran Dave Krieg. Detroit rallied to finish the season 9–7 and make the playoffs. But the Lions lost in the wild-card round to the Packers again. This time it was 16–12 in Green Bay. Sanders rushed for minus-1 yard on 13 carries.

The 1995 Lions started just 3–6. Team owner William Clay Ford Sr. issued an ultimatum: make the playoffs, or there would be big changes, starting with Fontes.

The Lions responded well. Mitchell passed for 410 yards and four touchdowns to lead Detroit to a 44–38 win over the Minnesota Vikings in November. Mitchell broke Bobby Layne's 45-year-old team record of 374 passing yards in a game.

Detroit won its final seven regular-season games in 1995 to finish 10–6. That also earned them a wild-card spot in the play-offs. Dreams of the Super Bowl did not materialize, though. The visiting Lions lost 58–37 to the Philadelphia Eagles. It was the highest-scoring playoff game in NFL history at the time. That record of 95 combined points was broken in 2010, when the Pack-ers beat the Arizona Cardinals 51–45.

Bobby Ross replaced Fontes as the Lions' head coach in 1997. That year, Sanders racked up 2,053 rushing yards. He became the third player in NFL history to rush for 2,000 yards in a sea-son. Through 2009, three more players had accomplished that feat. The Lions finished the sea-son 9–7. They then lost 20–10 to the host Tampa Bay Buccaneers in a wild-card playoff game. Sanders rushed for 65 yards on 18 carries.

Sanders shocked the foot-ball world when he retired in July 1999. He was only 31 years old and needed just 1,457 yards to pass former Chicago Bears star Walter Payton as the NFL's all-time leading rusher. Through 2009, Sanders ranked third in league history with 15,269 rush-ing yards. Only Emmitt Smith (18,355) and Payton (16,726) had more.

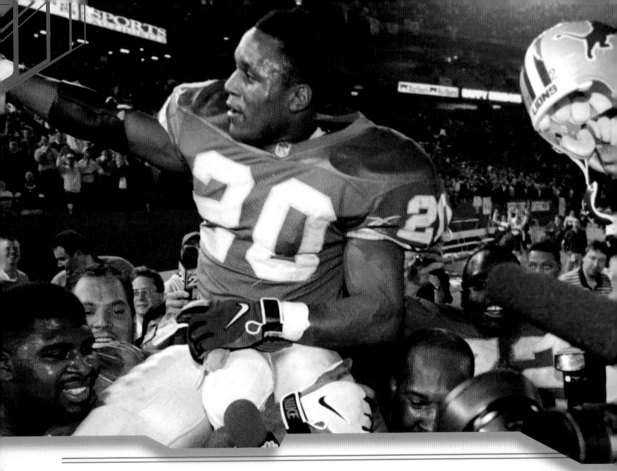

LIONS PLAYERS CARRY BARRY SANDERS AFTER HE RUSHED FOR 184 YARDS AND THE GAME-WINNING TOUCHDOWN AGAINST THE NEW YORK JETS IN 1997.

For Sanders, retiring felt right. "I always told myself I would play this game as long as it was fun," he said. "When it became a job for me, I decided it was time to move on."

The 1999 Lions finished 8–8 but still reached the postseason. This gave Detroit six playoff teams in the 1990s. That set a team record for the most playoff appearances in a 10-year span. Detroit lost again, though, falling 27–13 at Washington in the wild-card round.

CHAPTER 6
MILLEN'S MISTAKES

The 2000 Lions finished the season 9–7. They lost their final game 23–20 to the visiting Chicago Bears on a late field goal. As a result, Detroit did not make the playoffs. Unfortunately for the Lions, it would be their best season of the decade. The turn of a new century brought nothing but misery to the Lions. The 2000 through 2009 seasons were ones that the team's fans would like to forget.

Detroit vice chairman William Clay Ford Jr. hired Matt Millen as the team's president and CEO in January 2001. Millen would be responsible for deciding which players were on the Lions' roster and for building the team into a winner.

Millen had played 12 seasons in the NFL as a linebacker. He won four Super Bowls—two with the Raiders and one each with the 49ers and Redskins. He retired after the 1991 season. He then became a football commentator on television. When the

LIONS QUARTERBACK DAN ORLOVSKY WALKS OFF THE FIELD IN 2008 AFTER DETROIT BECAME THE FIRST TEAM TO GO WINLESS IN A 16-GAME SEASON.

FORD FIELD

The Lions moved into Ford Field, a beautiful new stadium in downtown Detroit, in 2002. In 1996, residents in Wayne County had voted to use public money to help the Lions build the indoor stadium. It would be located next to Comerica Park, a new baseball park for the Detroit Tigers. Ford Field's design incorporated the old Hudson's Department Store warehouse that had been in that location. The stadium includes large glass walls that allow natural light inside.

The Lions lost 37–31 to Green Bay on September 22, 2002, in the first regular-season game at Ford Field. Detroit picked up its first win at the stadium the next week, 26–21 over the New Orleans Saints. On February 5, 2006, Ford Field hosted Super Bowl XL between Pittsburgh and Seattle. The Steelers won 21–10. Pittsburgh running back Jerome Bettis retired after the game, going out on top in his hometown of Detroit.

Lions hired him, Millen had no front office experience.

Hiring Millen proved to be a disaster. During his seven seasons in control (2001–07), the Lions went 31–81 and owned the NFL's worst winning percentage at .277. They did not have a winning season. They never finished higher than third place in their division.

On February 4, 2003, Lions fans had thought that the team's struggles might be coming to an end. That was the day Michigan native Steve Mariucci became the twenty-second coach of the team. He signed a five-year, $25 million guaranteed contract.

Mariucci had been a successful head coach with the San Francisco 49ers from 1997 to 2002. The Lions and their fans believed that Mariucci was the right man to turn the

ANGRY DETROIT LIONS' FANS MARCH AROUND FORD FIELD DEMANDING
THAT THE LIONS FIRE TEAM PRESIDENT AND CEO MATT MILLEN IN 2005.

team around. But it was not to be. During Mariucci's two-plus seasons in Detroit, the Lions went a disappointing 15–28. The team did not come close to making the playoffs. Mariucci was fired midway through the 2005 season. Many Lions

HOMESICK

The Lions went the entire 2001, 2002, and 2003 seasons without a victory away from home. That made them the first team in NFL history not to win on the road for three consecutive seasons. The 24-game road losing streak came to an end on September 12, 2004, when the Lions defeated the Chicago Bears 20–16 at Soldier Field.

FROM LEFT TO RIGHT: WIDE RECEIVERS ROY WILLIAMS, MIKE WILLIAMS, AND CHARLES ROGERS NEVER LIVED UP TO EXPECTATIONS IN DETROIT.

followers were upset that Millen was not the one let go.

Some of the team's fans began a "Fire Millen" movement. It is thought to have started on December 10, 2005. A college basketball game was taking place between Michigan State and Wichita State at the Palace of Auburn Hills in suburban Detroit. An image of Mariucci appeared on the big screen. The fans proceeded to give Mariucci a standing ovation. Then they began chanting "Fire Millen!" Soon, the chant was heard at Detroit Pistons basketball games, Detroit Red Wings hockey games, and even at a Bulls basketball game in Chicago, Illinois.

Despite the fans' protests, the team did not dismiss Millen. He had received a five-year contract extension at the start of the 2005 season from owner William Clay Ford Sr. The Lions continued to struggle.

One of the main reasons the team's fans were angry at Millen was that he made poor decisions in the NFL Draft. In 2002, the team selected former University of Oregon quarterback Joey Harrington with the third overall pick. Harrington became Detroit's starter almost immediately. But his time with the Lions, from 2002 to 2005, was unsuccessful. Millen also made the unusual choice to select wide receivers in the first round three straight years—Charles Rogers

(2003), Roy Williams (2004), and Mike Williams (2005). Roy Williams played fairly well. But Mike Williams and Rogers did not.

Partly because of these poor draft decisions, Detroit did not improve. Defensive coordinator Dick Jauron was promoted to temporary head coach after Mariucci was fired. The Lions finished the 2005 season 5–11. They hired Rod Marinelli as coach in the offseason. But the losing records continued.

The Lions hit rock bottom during the 2008 season. Millen was fired after the team lost its first three games. Drivers of vehicles going past the team's practice facility beeped their horns and excitedly yelled about Millen's dismissal.

Millen's firing, however, did not improve the results on the field. In fact, Detroit lost all 16 of its games in 2008. This was the first time an NFL team finished 0–16. Tampa Bay had gone 0–14 in 1976. The league went to a 16-game schedule in 1978.

"It's just kind of numb," Lions veteran kicker Jason Hanson said after the team lost 0–16 season. "It's here. It's been coming, though, a train rolling down the tracks for a while. We tried to stop it. We couldn't."

QB CONNECTION

In early 2009, Matthew Stafford received a phone call from his mother asking, "Have you heard the story about Bobby Layne?" Though Stafford knew nothing about the "curse," he knew plenty about Layne. That is because Stafford had walked past two plaques at the entrance to Highland Park High School Stadium before each game for four years. Stafford played for the same high school in Dallas, Texas, as former Lions greats Layne and Doak Walker had decades previously. In 2005, Stafford led Highland Park to its first state championship in nearly 50 years.

Marinelli was fired as coach the next day. During his three seasons in charge, the Lions went 10–38. The Lions hired Jim Schwartz as his replacement. Schwartz had been the Tennessee Titans' defensive coordinator. He had helped the Titans go 13–3 in 2008. Detroit also hired former NFL head coaches Scott Linehan as offensive coordinator and Gunther Cunningham as defensive coordinator.

The rebuilding process continued with the 2009 NFL Draft. The Lions selected quarterback Matthew Stafford with the number one overall pick. The Lions broke a 19-game losing streak on September 27, 2009. They beat the Washington Redskins 19–14 at Ford Field. The Lions won only one other game in 2009.

Still, there were some positive signs for the Lions as the 2009 season came to an end.

LIONS RECEIVER CALVIN JOHNSON LOOKS FOR EXTRA YARDAGE AFTER A REVERSE PLAY AGAINST THE CHICAGO BEARS IN JANUARY 2010.

Stafford and wide receiver Calvin Johnson seemed to be forming a solid combination. The Lions had drafted Johnson second overall in 2007. Unlike the other wide receivers Detroit drafted that decade, the 6-foot-5, 235-pound Johnson appeared to be headed toward a standout pro football career.

If Bobby Layne did put a curse on the Lions, the 50 years were up in 2008. The city of Detroit, the Lions' organization, and the fans hope for the next 50 years to be as lucky as the previous 50 were unlucky.

TIMELINE

1929	The Portsmouth Spartans, based in Portsmouth, Ohio, begin play as an independent professional team. They join the NFL one year later.
1934	The Spartans are purchased and are moved to Detroit. The team name is changed to Lions.
1935	Quarterback Dutch Clark leads the Lions to a 26–7 win over the New York Giants in the NFL Championship Game.
1952	Behind quarterback Bobby Layne, the Lions win their second NFL championship, 17–7 over the Cleveland Browns.
1953	The Lions finish 10–2 and earn another spot in the NFL Championship Game. They again defeat the Browns—this time 17–16 in front of their Detroit fans.
1954	Detroit makes another trip to the NFL Championship Game against Cleveland. But the host Browns roll to a 56–10 win.
1957	The Lions advance to yet another NFL title game against the Browns. Detroit crushes Cleveland 59–14 in front of 55,263 fans at Briggs Stadium.
1958	Bobby Layne is traded to the Pittsburgh Steelers. On his way out of Detroit, Layne reportedly said the Lions would "not win for 50 years." It is later called the "Curse of Bobby Layne."
1970	The Lions qualify for the playoffs as the NFC's wild card. It is the first time the team reached the postseason since 1957. Detroit loses 5–0 to the Dallas Cowboys.

1975	The Lions begin a new era by playing their home games in the Silverdome in the Detroit suburb of Pontiac, Michigan.
1983	The Lions capture their first division championship since 1957. The host San Francisco 49ers beat the Lions 24–23 in the first round of the playoffs.
1989	Detroit drafts running back Barry Sanders out of Oklahoma State University with the third overall pick.
1992	Following the 1992 season, the Lions defeat the visiting Dallas Cowboys in the divisional round of the playoffs. On January 12, 1993, the Lions fall 41–10 to the host Washington Redskins in the NFC Championship Game.
1997	Sanders runs for 2,053 yards, becoming only the third player in NFL history, at the time, to reach 2,000 rushing yards in a season.
1999	Sanders retires before training camp. He is 31 years old and still in the prime of his career.
2002	The Lions move into a new stadium, Ford Field, in downtown Detroit.
2008	The Lions finish the season 0–16, becoming the first team to do so since the NFL went to a 16-game schedule in 1978.
2009	The Lions select quarterback Matthew Stafford with the number one pick in the NFL Draft. Detroit ends its 19-game losing streak with a 19–14 victory over Washington at Ford Field on September 27.

QUICK STATS

FRANCHISE HISTORY
Portsmouth Spartans (1930–33)
Detroit Lions (1934–)

SUPER BOWLS
(wins in bold)

None

NFL CHAMPIONSHIP GAMES
(1933–69; wins in bold)

1935, **1952**, **1953**, 1954, **1957**

NFC CHAMPIONSHIP GAMES
(since 1970 AFL-NFL merger)

1991

DIVISION CHAMPIONSHIPS
(since 1970 AFL-NFL merger)

1983, 1991, 1993

KEY PLAYERS
(position, seasons with team)

Lem Barney (DB, 1967–77)
Jack Christiansen (DB, 1951–58)
Dutch Clark (QB/K, 1931–38)
Lou Creekmur (OL, 1950–59)
Alex Karras (DT, 1958–70)
Dick Lane (DB, 1960–65)
Yale Lary (DB/P; 1952–53, 1956–64)
Bobby Layne (QB, 1950–58)
Dick LeBeau (DB, 1959–72)
Barry Sanders (RB, 1989–98)
Charlie Sanders (TE, 1968–77)
Joe Schmidt (LB, 1953–65)
Doak Walker (HB/K/P, 1950–55)
Alex Wojciechowicz (C/DE, 1938–46)

KEY COACHES
Buddy Parker (1951–56):
    47–23–2; 3–1 (playoffs)
George Wilson (1957–64):
    53–45–6; 2–0 (playoffs)

HOME FIELDS
Ford Field (2002–)
Pontiac Silverdome (1975–2001)
Tiger Stadium (1938–39, 1941–74)
    Known as Briggs Stadium 1938–60
University of Detroit Stadium
    (1934–37, 1940)
Universal Stadium (1930–33)

* All statistics through 2009 season

QUOTES AND ANECDOTES

Byron "Whizzer" White, who would later become a justice on the U.S. Supreme Court, played running back for Detroit in 1940 and 1941. In 1940, he became the first Lion to win the NFL's rushing title with 514 yards. White was a football star at the University of Colorado. He was drafted fourth overall by the NFL's Pittsburgh Pirates in 1938. White led the league in rushing as a rookie that year with 567 yards. After he deferred a Rhodes Scholarship for a year after college, he enrolled at Hertford College in England on the scholarship in 1939. He returned to the NFL with Detroit in 1940. His last season with the Lions, and in the NFL, was in 1941. He entered the U.S. Navy during World War II. After the war, he enrolled in Yale Law School rather than return to football. White practiced law in Denver, Colorado, and then, in 1962, he was appointed to the Supreme Court by President John F. Kennedy. White served on the court until his retirement in 1993. He died in Denver in 2002 at the age of 84 from complications from pneumonia.

Detroit quarterback Bobby Layne did not like sharing his job with the newly acquired Tobin Rote in 1957. Layne had led the Lions to NFL titles in 1952 and 1953 and had a lot of pride. He was not going to let Rote simply take the quarterback job from him. "One time we had a tough game in Chicago and were splitting time," Layne recalled. "I got knocked groggy and, laying there on the ground, I looked over at the bench and saw Tobin standing up and getting ready. I told myself, 'Let's go, Bobby. There's Rote waiting to take your bread and butter.' So I got up."

Lions standout defensive tackle Alex Karras had very poor eyesight. He wore thick glasses off the field. But he refused to wear them when he played.

GLOSSARY

comeback

Coming from behind to win a particular game.

contract

A binding agreement about, for example, years of commitment by a football player in exchange for a given salary.

coordinator

The top coaches overseeing the offense and defense of a team. Assistant coaches in charge of specific areas, like quarterbacks or linebackers, report to the coordinators.

draft

A system used by professional sports leagues to select new players in order to spread incoming talent among all teams.

hall of fame

A place built to honor noteworthy achievements by athletes in their respective sports.

Heisman Trophy

An award given to the top college football player each year.

juke

A deceptive move to get around an opponent.

playoffs

Games played to eliminate teams until a champion is determined.

retire

To officially end one's career.

rookie

A first-year professional player.

wild card

Playoff berths given to the best remaining teams that did not win their respective divisions.

FOR MORE INFORMATION

Further Reading

Plimpton, George. *Paper Lion: Confessions of a Last-String Quarterback*. Guilford, CT: The Lyons Press, 1965, 2009.

Sanders, Barry. *Barry Sanders Now You See Him: His Story in His Own Words*. Cincinnati, OH: Emmis Books, 2003.

Sanders, Charlie, with Larry Paladino. *Charlie Sanders' Tales from the Detroit Lions*. Champaign, IL: Sports Publishing LLC, 2005.

Web Links

To learn more about the Detroit Lions, visit ABDO Publishing Company online at **www.abdopublishing.com**. Web sites about the Lions are featured on our Book Links page. These links are routinely monitored and updated to provide the most current information available.

Places to Visit

Detroit Lions Headquarters and Training Facility
222 Republic Drive
Allen Park, MI 48101
313-262-2009
www.detroitlions.com/ford-field/practice-facility.html
This is the year-round team headquarters for the Lions. The public can watch the team at open practice sessions during training camp here.

Ford Field
2000 Brush Street
Detroit, MI 48226-2251
313-956-7824
www.detroitlions.com/ford-field
Ford Field has been the Lions' home stadium since 2002.

Pro Football Hall of Fame
2121 George Halas Drive, NW
Canton, OH 44708
330-456-8207
www.profootballhof.com
This hall of fame and museum highlights the greatest players and moments in the history of the National Football League. Eighteen people affiliated with the Lions are enshrined, including Dutch Clark, Bobby Layne, and Barry Sanders.

INDEX

About the Author

Matt Tustison specializes in editing and writing sports content at Red Line Editorial, Inc., in Burnsville, Minnesota. He previously worked as a sports copy editor at the *Baltimore Sun* and the *St. Paul Pioneer Press*, and he also has served as a freelance sports reporter for the Associated Press in Minneapolis. He graduated summa cum laude with a degree in Print Journalism from the University of St. Thomas in 2001 in his native St. Paul.